# Healthy Cooking
## for
## Primary Schools

### Sandra Mulvany

**Brilliant Publications**

Book 1

# Publisher's Information

Published by Brilliant Publications
Unit 10,
Sparrow Hall Farm,
Edlesborough,
Dunstable,
Bedfordshire,
LU6 2ES

Sales and stock enquiries:
Tel:      01202 712910
Fax:     0845 1309300
e-mail:   brilliant@bebc.co.uk
website:  www.brilliantpublications.co.uk

General information enquiries:
Tel:      01525 222292

The name "Brilliant Publications"
and the logo are registered trade marks.

Written by Sandra Mulvany
Illustrated by Kerry Ingham
Cover design by Brilliant Publications
Photography by Brilliant Publications
Printed in the UK

Other cooking books in this range are:
Healthy Cooking for Primary Schools (Book 2)
ISBN 978-1-905780-20-4
www.brilliantpublications.co.uk/PAGE1020

Healthy Cooking for Primary Schools (Book 3)
ISBN 978-1-905780-21-1
www.brilliantpublications.co.uk/PAGE1021

Healthy Cooking for Primary Schools (Book 4)
ISBN 978-1-905780-22-8
www.brilliantpublications.co.uk/PAGE1022

Healthy Cooking for Primary Schools (Book 5)
ISBN 978-1-905780-23-5
www.brilliantpublications.co.uk/PAGE1023

© 2008 Sandra Mulvany (text); Brilliant Publications (photography, design and layout)
ISBN  978-1-905780-19-8
First published 2008
10  9  8  7  6  5  4  3  2  1

The right of Sandra Mulvany to be identified as the author of this work has been asserted by herself in accordance with the Copyright, Design and Patents Act 1988.

*Healthy Cooking for Primary Schools (Book 1)* is photocopiable from page 7 through to page 87. These pages have the phrase 'This page may be photocopied for use by the purchasing institution only' at the bottom. They may be photocopied by the purchasing institution or individual teachers for classroom use only, without consent from the publisher. The material in this book may not be reproduced in any other form or for any other purpose without the prior permission of the publisher.

# Contents

Introduction .................................................................................................................. 5
How to Use the Resources ........................................................................................... 6
Visual Lesson Structure Cards ............................................................................... 7–10
Working Together: Discussion Cards .................................................................. 11–12

| Lesson | Recipe | Teaching Point | Learning Objective | |
|--------|--------|----------------|---------------------|---|
| 1 | Fruit Salad | | | 13–18 |
| | | Skill | How to Cut | 14 |
| | | Theory | Food and Us | 15 |
| | | Health and Safety | Washing Your Hands | 15 |
| 2 | Rainbow Sticks | | | 19–24 |
| | | Skill | How to Put Food on Skewers | 20 |
| | | Theory | About Vitmin C | 21 |
| | | Health and Safety | Cleaning Your Nails | 21 |
| 3 | Pitta Bread Filling | | | 25–30 |
| | | Skill | How to Wash Fruit and Vegetables | 26 |
| | | Theory | Why Wash Fruit and Vegetables? | 27 |
| | | Health and Safety | Advantages of an Apron | 27 |
| 4 | Fruit Smoothie | | | 31–36 |
| | | Skill | How to Remove Strawberry Stalks | 32 |
| | | Theory | About Bananas | 33 |
| | | Health and Safety | Using a Blender Safely | 33 |
| 5 | Bread Pizza | | | 37–42 |
| | | Skill | How to Spread | 38 |
| | | Theory | Where Does Flour Come From? | 39 |
| | | Health and Safety | Reasons to Tie Back our Hair | 39 |
| 6 | Afternoon Tea Bread | | | 43–48 |
| | | Skill | How to Weigh Ingredients | 44 |
| | | Theory | Types of Flour – Which is Healthier? | 45 |
| | | Health and Safety | Reasons to Avoid Dangly Sleeves | 45 |

© Sandra Mulvany and Brilliant Publications     **Healthy Cooking for Primary Schools (Book 1)**

# Contents (cont.)

| Lesson | Recipe | Teaching Point | Learning Objective | |
|---|---|---|---|---|
| 7 | Cous Cous Salad | | | 49–54 |
| | | Skill | How to Sprinke | 50 |
| | | Theory | What is Cous Cous? | 51 |
| | | Health and Safety | Reasons to Close Cupboard Doors | 51 |
| 8 | Irish Soda Bread | | | 55–60 |
| | | Skill | How to Turn the Oven On | 56 |
| | | Theory | When is the Oven Hot Enough? | 57 |
| | | Health and Safety | Gas Ovens Are Dangerous | 57 |
| 9 | Pizza | | | 61–66 |
| | | Skill | How to Roll Out | 62 |
| | | Theory | About Carbohydrates | 63 |
| | | Health and Safety | Realizing Knives are Sharp | 63 |
| 10 | Welsh Rarebit | | | 67–72 |
| | | Skill | How to Use a Grill | 68 |
| | | Theory | About Calcium | 69 |
| | | Health and Safety | Reasons to Avoid Running Around | 69 |
| 11 | Chinese Noodle Soup | | | 73–78 |
| | | Skill | How to Squeeze a Lemon | 74 |
| | | Theory | Noodles: How They Are Made | 75 |
| | | Health and Safety | Stirring Hot Liquid Safely | 75 |
| 12 | Danish Frikadeller | | | 79–84 |
| | | Skill | How to Turn Food Over | 80 |
| | | Theory | Lean or Fat Meat. Which is Better? | 81 |
| | | Health and Safety | Reasons for Keeping Your Hands Clean | 81 |

What Can You Remember? (1) ..................................................................85
What Can You Remember? (2) ..................................................................86
Certificate of Achievement........................................................................87

**Healthy Cooking for Primary Schools (Book 1)**

# Introduction

Healthy Cooking for Primary Schools (Book 1) is part of a series of five books, providing a practical cooking programme for primary schools. Each book contains 12 easy-to-follow recipes.

For each recipe you will find:

Skill focus for lesson – These become progressively more advanced as you progress through the series

Theory – Providing information on where food comes from, nutrition, balanced diet and healthy eating

Health and safety points.

Each recipe appears in two formats, so that you can choose the format best suited to your pupils' reading abilities:

Illustrated step-by-step format

Traditional format

The instructions are exactly the same in both versions, so you may use both in mixed ability classes.

The assessment sheets on pages 85 and 86 provide a fun way of testing the practical and theoretical knowledge gained.

The Certificate of Achievement on page 87 can either be used as an ongoing record or be given out when all the recipes in the book have been completed.

The book is fully photocopiable from pages 7–87 inclusive, allowing you maximum user flexibility.

# How to Use the Resources

How to Use the Resources
All ingredients are based on two pupils sharing, and the timings will all fit into a double lesson of approximately 80 minutes. We recommend you use low-fat options where possible.

Make a display using the Visual Lesson Structure Cards (pages 7–10) and pictures of the recipe and skill to be focussed on in the lesson (to download colour photos of the recipes, log on to www.brilliantpublications.co.uk/PAGE1019 and click on the recipe you want).

Keep the skill, theory and health and safety point sheets to hand so that you can refer to them when demonstrating to pupils. (The language has been kept as simple as possible on these sheets, so you may wish to give copies to your pupils as well.)

Choose the best format of the recipe to use for each pair of children and photocopy sufficient copies. The illustrated versions of the recipes can be photocopied onto either an A3 sheet (if space is an issue, fold it in half so that you view six steps at a time), or reduced to A4 size.

If you place the recipes and other sheets in clear plastic wallets (or laminate them), they can be used again and again.

Encourage children to gather together all the ingredients and equipment they need before starting. They could tick things off on their copy of the recipe.

Demonstrate the recipe 2–3 steps at a time, introducing the skill, theory and health and safety points as you progress through the recipe.

An important aspect of learning to cook is learning to work together. You may wish to display the Discussion cards on pages 11–12 (Communicate, Share, Help, Be pleasant) so that you can refer to these throughout the lesson.

Above all, have fun and enjoy cooking!

# Today We are Making

1

# Today We are Learning

2

# Read Recipe

## 3

# Wash Hands and Prepare

## 4

# Cook

5

# Clear Away

6

# Tasting

**7**

# We Have Learnt

**8**

# Communicate

It is vital to have good communication in the kitchen. If you are working with a partner, it is important to say what you are doing and to agree on who does what. You have to talk about what you would like to do and listen to what your partner wants to do. Then you have to work out a way to make it fair for both of you. You can only come to an agreement if you talk together!

You should also let others know if there are any dangers, such as you opening the oven or if water has been spilt on the floor. Talking is absolutely key to good cooking habits. The better you are at communicating, the better you are at cooking in a school kitchen.

# Share

Good sharing follows on from good communicating. If you have communicated well, you will have reached a fair decision about sharing. Sharing works best when it has been done fairly and everyone is happy. Sharing is particularly difficult if it involves doing something really exciting or really boring. You have to imagine that the other person feels very much like yourself. This can be hard to imagine, but it is an important lesson to learn. Sharing is a lot easier when you talk together about things.

# Help

It is important to be able to help others, but it is also important to accept help from others. Help is a two-way thing. If you are offering your help to someone else, it is important that you choose your words carefully. Be kind in giving your help, as it can be hard to accept help given with harsh words. If you have communicated well, you will be able to help each other well. If you are very capable, offer your help kindly, but also let others help you in return, even if it is to do with something you feel you might already know about.

# Be pleasant

It is, in fact, very simple to be pleasant. Look at and listen to the person you are working with and notice something he or she does well. Then say something pleasant about that. You will soon discover that the more pleasant you are to people, the more pleasant they are back to you. You can also do something pleasant, like smile at a person or pat someone kindly on the back. Don't just wait for someone to be pleasant to you; try to be the first one to say or do something pleasant.

# Fruit Salad

# How to Cut

Knives are sharp and can cut you very easily. Always be careful when using a knife. If you touch the blade it can cut you. Always hold the knife by its handle and point the sharp blade down towards the table or cutting board. (If you wish, you can put a mark on the top of the knife to show you which edge of the blade is sharp.)

# Food and Us

Food serves the same function for us as fuel does for cars. Without food and water we simply couldn't live. Food is full of nutrients (vitamins, minerals and proteins) that our body needs to work properly. There are different types of nutrients and these are found in different types of food. We need a little bit of all the different nutrients and that's why we have to eat a little bit of many different types of food. Food isn't just about keeping us from being hungry and filling us up. It is about getting all the right kinds of nutrients to make all the bits of our body work.

# Washing Your Hands

It is important to wash your hands before you start cooking. This is to wash off any dirt and bacteria. You have to wash your hands with warm water and soap. You should make your hands wet, add soap and then rub your soapy hands together away from the water for at least 20 seconds. Then rinse thoroughly under the water and dry your hands with a disposable towel.

# Fruit Salad

**Ingredients:**

Tin of peaches   Banana   Green grapes
Strawberries   Raspberries   Satsuma

1. Wash fresh fruit.
2. Open tin of peaches.
3. Sieve juice into bowl.
4. Cut peaches and add to bowl.
5. Peel and cut banana and add to bowl.
6. Cut grapes and add to bowl.

# Fruit Salad (cont.)

**Equipment:**
Chopping board   Sharp knife   Tin opener
Bowl             Sieve

7. Remove leafy stalks from strawberries by twisting them.

8. Cut strawberries and add to bowl.

9. Add raspberries to bowl.

10. Peel satsuma.

11. Divide into segments and add to bowl.

12. Cover fruit salad and keep cool in fridge.

# Fruit Salad

**Ingredients:**
Tin of peaches
Banana
Green grapes
Strawberries
Raspberries
Satsuma

**Equipment:**
Chopping board
Sharp knife
Tin opener
Bowl
Sieve

**Instructions:**

1. Wash fresh fruit.

2. Open tin of peaches.

3. Sieve juice into bowl.

4. Cut peaches and add to bowl.

5. Peel and cut banana and add to bowl.

6. Cut grapes and add to bowl.

7. Remove leafy stalks from strawberries by twisting them.

8. Cut strawberries and add to bowl.

9. Add raspberries to bowl.

10. Peel satsuma.

11. Divide into segments and add to bowl.

12. Cover fruit salad and keep cool in fridge.

# Rainbow Sticks

# How to Put Food on Skewers

A skewer has one very sharp end. Therefore, be careful when you thread something onto a skewer. Hold the skewer carefully with one hand and hold the food between your fingers and thumb. Then thread the food on gently, making sure that the palm of your hand is to the side of the skewer.

**Healthy Cooking for Primary Schools (Book 1)**

www.brilliantpublications.co.uk

© Sandra Mulvany and Brilliant Publications

This page may be photocopied by the purchasing institution only.

# About Vitamin C

There are many types of vitamins, such as vitamins A, B, C, D, E and K. Vitamins are a type of nutrient which the body needs. Fruit and vegetables are excellent sources of all vitamins – especially vitamin C. Vitamin C plays a very important protective role in the body. Unlike most animals, humans cannot produce vitamin C, so we need it in our diet. Although we need only a small amount of vitamin C, we cannot store it in our bodies and so we have to eat food rich in vitamin C on a regular basis.

# Cleaning Your Nails

Remember that dirt is often trapped under your nails. Therefore, have a good look under your nails when you wash your hands. If they are dirty, you will have to clean them. You can use a nail brush or a nail file.

# Rainbow Sticks

**Ingredients:** Green grapes   Banana   Mangetout
Dried apricot   Mushrooms   Cherry tomatoes
Pineapple chunks

1. Wash all fruit and vegetables.

2. Peel banana.

3. Cut banana into small chunks.

4. Open tin of pineapple chunks.

5. Drain into a sieve.

6. Put a grape on a skewer.

# Rainbow Sticks (cont.)

**Equipment:**
Chopping board   Tin opener   Sharp knife
Sieve            Wooden skewers

7. Then put on a cherry tomato.

8. Put a mushroom on the skewer.

9. Fold mangetout around a pineapple chunk and put on.

10. Put on a banana chunk and a dried apricot.

11. Finish off with a grape.

12. Make your own design.

© Sandra Mulvany and Brilliant Publications
This page may be photocopied by the purchasing institution only.

**Healthy Cooking for Primary Schools (Book 1)**
www.brilliantpublications.co.uk

# Rainbow Sticks

**Ingredients:**
Green grapes
Banana
Mangetout
Dried apricot
Cherry tomatoes
Mushrooms
Pineapple chunks

**Equipment:**
Chopping board
Tin opener
Sharp knife
Sieve
Wooden skewers

**Instructions:**

1. Wash all fruit and vegetables.

2. Peel banana.

3. Cut banana into small chunks.

4. Open tin of pineapple chunks.

5. Drain into a sieve.

6. Put a grape on the skewer.

7. Then put on a cherry tomato.

8. Put a mushroom on the skewer.

9. Fold mangetout around a pineapple chunk and put on.

10. Put on a banana chunk and a dried apricot.

11. Finish off with a grape.

12. Make you own design.

# Pitta Bread Filling

# How to Wash Fruit and Vegetables

It is important to wash vegetables before your prepare them. It is a good idea to cut off the bits we obviously don't need before washing them. (For example, cut off the green tops of carrots before you wash them). You can put the vegetables in a colander if you want. Hold them under a cold tap and scrub them with your hands. You can also use a vegetable brush on harder vegetables.

# Why Wash Fruit and Vegetables?

Washing vegetables in water removes nearly all dirt, insects and bacteria. Remember that even if you grow your own vegetables, they will be full of dirt. Also remember that if you buy vegetables loose in a shop, other people may have touched them or even coughed or sneezed over them.

# Advantages of an Apron

Always use an apron when you are preparing food or cooking. This is to avoid getting your clothes dirty. It also avoids any dirt from your clothes falling into the food. There are many types of aprons but the most common type slips over the head and ties around the back. Some people find it hard to tie a knot behind their back – have patience, it takes practice.

# Pitta Bread Filling

**Ingredients:**
Pitta bread   Cucumber   Dressing   Baby corn
Iceberg lettuce   Cherry tomatoes   Mushrooms

1. Wash the vegetables.

2. Cut off any bad spots.

3. Cut cucumber with Claw Method.

4. Cut baby corn with Claw Method.

5. Cut mushrooms in half with Bridge Method.

6. Put flat side down and slice.

**Healthy Cooking for Primary Schools (Book 1)**

# Pitta Bread Filling (cont.)

**Equipment:**
Chopping board   Sharp knife   Mixing bowl
Mixing spoon     Baking tray

7. Halve cherry tomatoes and halve again.

8. Cut the lettuce.

9. Put in all in the bowl.

10. Add dressing and mix it in.

11. Heat up pitta bread.

12. Cut a heated pitta bread open and add the salad.

© Sandra Mulvany and Brilliant Publications
This page may be photocopied by the purchasing institution only.

**Healthy Cooking for Primary Schools (Book 1)**
www.brilliantpublications.co.uk

# Pitta Bread Filling

**Ingredients:**
Pitta bread
Dressing
Iceberg lettuce
Mushrooms
Cherry tomatoes
Cucumber
Baby corn

**Equipment:**
Chopping board
Sharp knife
Mixing bowl
Mixing spoon
Baking tray

**Instructions:**

1. Wash the vegetables.

2. Cut off any bad spots.

3. Cut cucumber with Claw Method.

4. Cut baby corn with Claw Method.

5. Cut mushrooms in half with Bridge Method.

6. Put flat side down and slice them.

7. Halve cherry tomatoes and halve again.

8. Cut the lettuce.

9. Put it all in a bowl.

10. Add dressing and mix it in.

11. Heat up pitta bread.

12. Cut a heated pitta bread open and add the salad.

**TIP**
Your teacher might heat up the pitta breads for the whole class.

# Fruit Smoothie

Decorated with coloured sugar, strawberry and umbrella.

# How to Remove Strawberry Stalks

If you want to take the leafy-green top off a strawberry, you have to hold onto the strawberry with one hand, whilst you twist the top gently with the other hand. If the fruit is ripe, the leafy-green top should come off easily with the white centre of the strawberry. Do it firmly, but carefully, as you do not want to crush the strawberry.

# About Bananas

Bananas grow in the Tropics, which is the area centred on the equator. In particular, Ecuador, Costa Rica, the Philippines and Colombia are big exporters of bananas. Bananas grow in clusters on very tall plants that grow as high as 8 metres, with leaves as long as 3.5 metres. The bananas we find in our supermarkets are normally picked when they are still green. They are then only ripened when they arrive at their destination.

# Using a Blender Safely

Be very careful when you use any type of blender. These are electrical machines with sharp parts, so you can imagine how dangerous they can be. Always make sure that the lid is tightly fitted before you start. This will avoid the food going everywhere. Also make sure that the electrical cord is in a good state of repair. When you are first learning to use a blender, you must let an adult help you. Always remember to keep electrical appliances away from water and never use them while you have wet hands.

# Fruit Smoothie

**Ingredients:**

4 strawberries  1 banana  1 nectarine
150ml strawberry yogurt  150ml orange juice

1. Take the leafy-green tops off the strawberries.

2. Wash the strawberries and the nectarine.

3. Cut the strawberries in half.

4. Peel the banana.

5. Chop the banana.

6. Cut the nectarine in half.

# Fruit Smoothie (cont.)

**Equipment:**
Chopping board    Knife    Measuring jug    Blender
2 glasses

7. Take the stone out of the nectarine.

8. Cut the nectarine.

9. Add the fruit to the blender.

10. Add the yogurt to the blender.

11. Add the orange juice to the blender.

12. Put the lid on and blend. Pour into the glasses.

# Fruit Smoothie

**Ingredients:**
4 strawberries
1 banana
1 nectarine
150ml strawberry yogurt
150ml orange juice

**Equipment:**
Chopping board
Knife
Measuring jug
Blender
2 glasses

**Instructions:**

1. Take the leafy-green tops off the strawberries.

2. Wash the strawberries and the nectarine.

3. Cut the strawberries in half.

4. Peel the banana.

5. Chop the banana.

6. Cut the nectarine in half.

7. Take the stone out of the nectarine.

8. Cut the nectarine.

9. Add the fruit to the blender.

10. Add the yogurt to the blender.

11. Add the orange juice to the blender.

12. Put the lid on and blend. Pour into the glasses.

# Bread Pizza

# How to Spread

When you spread anything on a piece of bread, make sure that the angle of the knife is right. Support the bread with one hand and spread with the other. Make sure to spread evenly and right out to the edges.

# Where Does Flour Come From?

The flour we use in baking normally comes from wheat. Wheat is a type of cereal that farmers grow in their fields in the summer. It looks golden when it is ripe for harvesting. After harvesting, the grains get milled and this is how flour is produced.

There are many varieties of flour, wholemeal, brown and white being the main types. Wholemeal flour is where the whole grain is used. Brown flour uses about 85% of the kernel, removing some of the outer part (known as bran). White flour only uses the central part, or endosperm, removing most of the wheat grain's nutrients altogether.

# Reasons to Tie Back our Hair

Always put your hair up if you have long hair. It is unhygienic to have your long hair loose in the kitchen. Your hair can also get caught in appliances or even catch fire, not to mention loose hair falling out in the food.

# Bread Pizza

**Ingredients:**
Slice of brown bread
2 spring onions
2–3 tbsp tomato purée
2 slices of ham
50g cheese

1. Put the oven on 190°C.

2. Get all your equipment out.

3. Place a small saucer on the bread.

4. Cut around to make a circle.

5. Spread purée on the circle of bread.

6. Cut the ham.

# Bread Pizza (cont.)

**Equipment:**
Small saucer   Butter knife   Chopping board   Scales
Sharp knife    Baking tray    Grater           Tablespoon

7. Put the ham on the bread.

8. Chop the spring onion.

9. Put spring onion on the bread.

10. Weigh and grate the cheese.

11. Sprinkle the cheese on.

12. Bake for 10–15 minutes.

© Sandra Mulvany and Brilliant Publications
This page may be photocopied by the purchasing institution only.

**Healthy Cooking for Primary Schools (Book 1)**
www.brilliantpublications.co.uk

# Bread Pizza

**Ingredients:**
Slice of brown bread
2–3 tbsp tomato purée
2 spring onion
2 slices of ham
50g cheese

**Equipment:**
Small saucer
Butter knife
Chopping board
Sharp knife
Baking tray
Grater
Tablespoon
Scales

**Instructions:**

1. Put the oven on 190°C.

2. Get all your equipment out.

3. Place a small saucer on the bread.

4. Cut around to make a circle.

5. Spread purée on the circle of bread.

6. Cut the ham.

7. Put the ham on the bread.

8. Chop the spring onion.

9. Put spring onion on the bread.

10. Weigh and grate the cheese.

11. Sprinkle the cheese on.

12. Bake for 10–15 minutes.

# Afternoon Tea Bread

# How to Weigh Ingredients

**Skill**

You have to know your numbers to be able to weigh accurately. There are many types of weighing scales: electronic scales, scales with a dial and old-fashioned scales with balance and weights. They all require different skills. Remember that if you are using electronic scales, you must zero them first and make sure that you are measuring in grams (and not ounces). Also remember that you cannot take the bowl on and off if you are using electronic scales.

**Healthy Cooking for Primary Schools (Book 1)**

© Sandra Mulvany and Brilliant Publications

www.brilliantpublications.co.uk

This page may be photocopied by the purchasing institution only.

# Types of Flour – Which is Healthier?

Our baking flour is normally made from wheat. A grain of wheat consists of the bran, the wheatgerm and the endosperm. White flour is made by grinding only the endosperm. Brown flour is made by grinding about 85% of the grain. Wholemeal flour is made by grinding the whole grain, including all the bran and the wheatgerm which contain both fibre and vitamins B and E. This is why foods made using wholemeal flour are much healthier for us.

# Reasons to Avoid Dangly Sleeves

You must never wear dangly sleeves when you are working in the kitchen. Not only will they get dirty, but the sleeves can also easily get caught in appliances or even catch fire.

# Afternoon Tea Bread

**Ingredients:** 75g wholemeal flour   1 tsp baking powder
50g plain flour   25g margarine   1 tsp cinnamon
2 tsp sugar   ½ egg   75ml milk

1. Set oven to 200°C.

2. Weigh out the flours and margarine.

3. Combine the flours and rub in the margarine.

4. Add the sugar, cinnamon and baking powder.

5. Crack the egg into a cup.

6. Whisk the egg.

# Afternoon Tea Bread (cont.)

**Equipment:** Scales   Mixing bowl   Teaspoon
Mixing spoon   Whisk/fork   Cup   Measuring jug
Flour dredger   Rolling pin   Baking tray

7. Add the milk and ½ of the egg to the bowl.

8. Stir to mix together. Use hands to form a big ball.

9. Divide into 4 balls of dough on a floured surface.

10. Roll out each ball of dough.

11. Put on a greased baking tray.

12. Bake for 10–15 minutes.

# Afternoon Tea Bread

**You Will Need:**
75g wholemeal flour
50g plain flour
25g margarine
1 tsp baking powder
2 tsp sugar
1 tsp cinnamon
½ egg
75ml milk

**Equipment:**
Scales
Mixing bowl
Teaspoon
Mixing spoon
Egg whisk
Cup
Measuring jug
Baking tray
Rolling pin
Flour dredger

**Instructions:**

1. Set oven to 200°C.

2. Weigh out the flours and margarine.

3. Combine the flours and rub in the margarine.

4. Add the sugar, cinnamon and baking powder.

5. Crack the egg into a cup.

6. Whisk the egg.

7. Add the milk and ½ of the egg to the bowl.

8. Stir to mix together. Use hands to form a big ball.

9. Divide into 4 balls of dough on a floured surface.

10. Roll out each ball of dough.

11. Put on a greased baking tray.

12. Bake for 10–15 minutes.

**TIP**
Share 1 egg between 2 sets of partners after you have whisked it.

# Cous Cous Salad

# How to Sprinkle

When you sprinkle a stock cube, you simply have to rub and squeeze the cube between your fingers and let it sprinkle. Be careful when you have to sprinkle it into boiling water, as the steam can burn you. If possible, allow the saucepan to cool down slightly before you sprinkle or alternatively, sprinkle the cube into your hand and then add it carefully, but quickly, to the hot water.

# What is Cous Cous?

Cous cous is made from crushed wheat. For centuries it has been one of the main foods eaten in North African countries, namely Morocco, Algeria and Tunisia. Its bland flavour means that it tastes good with lots of different kinds of ingredients: spices, meats, vegetables or fruit. Traditionally, cous cous is made by a lengthy process of rolling, rubbing, sieving, moistening and drying the wheat. Nowadays, you can just buy it ready-made at the supermarket.

# Reasons to Close Cupboard Doors

Always close cupboard doors after you. This is because open cupboard doors are a hazard in the kitchen. You and other people could easily fall over an open low-cupboard door or bang your head on it if it's a higher door.

# Cous Cous Salad

**Ingredients:** 100g cous cous  1 tsp fresh coriander
200ml water  1 stock cube  4 cherry tomatoes
1 tbsp sultanas  4 sugar snap peas  4 baby sweet corn

1. Wash the vegetables.

2. Add 200ml water to a saucepan.

3. Bring the water to the boil.

4. Sprinkle in the stock cube.

5. Add the cous cous.

6. Put a lid on and take off the hob.

# Cous Cous Salad (cont.)

**Equipment:**
Scales
Mixing spoon
Measuring jug
Sharp knife
Saucepan and lid
Chopping board

7. Leave cous cous for 10 minutes.

8. Cut the tomatoes and sugar snap peas.

9. Cut the baby sweet corn.

10. Add it all to the cous cous and mix.

11. Chop the coriander.

12. Add the sultanas and coriander. Mix and serve.

# Cous Cous Salad

**Ingredients:**
100g cous cous
4 baby sweet corn
4 cherry tomatoes
4 sugar snap peas
200ml water
1 stock cube
1 tbsp sultanas
1 tsp fresh coriander

**Equipment:**
Scales
Measuring jug
Saucepan and lid
Mixing spoon
Sharp knife
Chopping board

**Instructions:**

1. Wash the vegetables.

2. Add 200ml water to a saucepan.

3. Bring the water to the boil.

4. Sprinkle in the stock cube.

5. Add the cous cous.

6. Put a lid on and take off the hob.

7. Leave cous cous for 10 minutes.

8. Cut the tomatoes and sugar snap peas.

9. Cut the baby sweet corn.

10. Add it all to the cous cous and mix.

11. Chop the coriander.

12. Add the sultanas and coriander. Mix and serve.

# Irish Soda Bread

# How to Turn the Oven on

You need to know your numbers in order to turn on an oven. An electric oven is easier to put on than a gas oven. With some electric ovens, you need to switch them on at the wall first. Then you need to find the right control knob and turn it to the correct temperature. The number you want may just be shown as a small dot between two other numbers. On some gas ovens, you must press the ignition to get a spark. Keep holding down the ignition button and turn the control knob. Do not let go of the ignition button until you have a flame.

# When is the Oven Hot Enough?

An oven takes a while to heat up to the right temperature. Most ovens have an indicator light next to the control knobs. This light will come on when you turn on the oven. It will go off when the temperature you chose has been reached.

# Gas Ovens Are Dangerous

Be VERY careful with gas ovens. You need a flame to burn off the gas. If there is no flame and the gas is coming out, the entire room will fill with gas. This is very dangerous. At the slightest spark, a room or house full of gas will explode with obvious consequences. Close gas oven doors carefully, otherwise the rush of air caused by the closing will put out the flame. Be aware of any smell of gas. If you discover that gas is coming out, you must turn the oven off straight away, open the windows and leave the room. Never try to ignite the oven with gas in the room.

If you should enter a room and smell gas, NEVER turn on the light switch as this can create a spark which can ignite the gas and cause an explosion.

# Irish Soda Bread

**Ingredients:** 100g wholemeal flour  100g plain flour
1 tsp bicarbonate of soda  1 tsp baking powder  ½ egg
1 tbsp brown sugar  150ml natural yogurt

1. Put the oven on 190°C.

2. Put the wholemeal flour in a bowl.

3. Add the plain flour and mix.

4. Add the baking powder and mix.

5. Add the bicarbonate of soda and mix.

6. Add the sugar and mix.

**Healthy Cooking for Primary Schools (Book 1)**

# Irish Soda Bread (cont.)

**Equipment:** Scales    Flour dredger
Measuring jug    Mixing bowl    Measuring spoons    Cup
Knife    Whisk/fork    Mixing spoon    Baking tray

7. Crack an egg into a cup and whisk.

8. Add half the egg to the yogurt.

9. Add this to the bowl and mix to form a dough.

10. Lightly knead on a floured surface and shape into 4 rolls.

11. Put on a baking tray and cut a cross in the top.

12. Bake for 10–15 minutes.

# Irish Soda Bread

**Ingredients:**
100g wholemeal flour
100g plain flour
1 tsp bicarbonate of soda
1 tsp baking powder
½ egg
1 tbsp brown sugar
150ml natural yogurt

**Equipment:**
Scales
Measuring jug
Cup
Whisk/fork
Baking tray
Baking tray

Flour dredger
Mixing bowl
Knife
Mixing spoon
Measuring spoons

**Instructions:**

1. Put the oven on 190°C.

2. Put the wholemeal flour in a bowl.

3. Add the plain flour and mix.

4. Add the baking powder and mix.

5. Add the bicarbonate of soda and mix.

6. Add the sugar and mix.

7. Crack an egg into a cup and whisk.

8. Add half the egg to the yogurt.

9. Add this to the bowl and mix to form a dough.

10. Lightly knead it on a floured surface and shape into 4 rolls.

11. Put on a baking tray and cut a cross in the top.

12. Bake for 10–15 minutes.

**TIP**
Share 1 egg between 2 sets of partners after you have whisked it.

# Pizza

# How to Roll out

Make sure that your dough isn't too sticky. If it is, add a bit more flour. Sprinkle a little flour onto the table and roll your rolling pin in it. Shape the dough into a ball and gently roll it out. Turn the dough over and keep turning it around so that you are rolling it into a circle. If the dough begins to stick, sprinkle a little more flour from the flour dredger over the rolling pin or over the dough.

# About Carbohydrates

Carbohydrates are found in wheat, oats, potatoes, rice or any food made from these, such as bread. These are starchy carbohydrates and they give you slow-releasing energy for work and warmth. Sugar is another type of carbohydrate. It gives you a quick rush of energy, but it doesn't last. Of course, sugar isn't good for your teeth, so stick with starchy carbohydrates.

# Realizing Knives are Sharp

Do not forget that knives are very sharp. If you touch the sharp blade, you can cut yourself. Always point the sharp blade down towards the table. You can always put a mark on the handle to show which side is safe and which side is sharp.

If you have to carry a sharp knife, you must be especially careful. Hold it firmly in your hand with the blade pointing straight down.

# Pizza

**Ingredients:**
Pepperoni
2–3 tbsp tomato purée
100g self-raising flour
25g margarine
½ tsp mixed herbs
Sweet corn
50ml milk
75g cheese

1. Put the oven on 200°C.

2. Sieve flour into bowl.

3. Rub in the margarine.

4. Add milk to form a dough.

5. Roll out to a circle on a floured surface.

6. Put dough on a greased baking tray.

# Pizza (cont.)

**Equipment:** Sharp knife   Mixing bowl   Scales   Sieve
Flour dredger   Teaspoon   Mixing spoon   Chopping board
Grater   Measuring jug   Rolling pin   Baking tray

7. Spread tomato purée over the pizza.

8. Sprinkle on some sweet corn.

9. Cut the pepperoni and put it on the pizza.

10. Grate the cheese and sprinkle over.

11. Sprinkle over the herbs.

12. Bake for 15–20 minutes.

© Sandra Mulvany and Brilliant Publications
This page may be photocopied by the purchasing institution only.

Healthy Cooking for Primary Schools (Book 1)
www.brilliantpublications.co.uk

# Pizza

**Ingredients:**
100g self-raising flour
Sweet corn
2–3 tbsp tomato purée
Pepperoni
25g margarine
50ml milk
½ tsp mixed herbs
75g cheese

**Equipment:**
Sharp knife
Teaspoon
Mixing spoon
Flour dredger
Grater
Rolling pin
Mixing bowl
Scales
Sieve
Chopping board
Measuring jug
Baking tray

**Instructions:**

1. Put oven on 200°C.

2. Sieve flour into bowl.

3. Rub in the margarine.

4. Add milk to form a dough.

5. Roll out to a circle on a floured surface.

6. Put dough on a greased baking tray.

7. Spread tomato purée over the pizza.

8. Sprinkle on some sweet corn.

9. Cut the pepperoni and put it on the pizza.

10. Grate the cheese and sprinkle over.

11. Sprinkle over the herbs.

12. Bake for 15–20 minutes.

# Welsh Rarebit

# How to Use a Grill

It can be dangerous using a grill. It gets very hot and it is normally placed inside an oven, making it awkward to get to. Normally, you also need to have the oven door open to use the grill, creating another hazard. Remember to pay attention when you are using the grill. A grill can take a while to heat up. When it is hot, slide the grill tray in carefully and bend down to keep an eye on it. Do not stand too close to it, as you may get burnt by spitting fat or food fragments.

# About Calcium

Calcium is a mineral found in milk. Therefore, calcium is found in anything made from milk, such as cheese and yogurt. Calcium is good for bones and teeth. Calcium is especially important for growing children, pregnant women and older people with weak bones.

# Reasons to Avoid Running Around

Never run in a kitchen. There are many hazards in a kitchen and you would be putting yourself and others in danger. If you are not careful and bump into someone, food can be spilled, burning someone if it is hot or making the floor slippery and hazardous.

# Welsh Rarebit

**Ingredients:**
2 slices of brown bread
2 tbsp milk
1 tomato
75g Cheddar cheese
1 tsp mustard
Butter to spread
Pinch of salt and pepper

**Equipment:**
Grater
Chopping board
Measuring spoons
Mixing spoon
Sharp knife
Mixing bowl
Knife
Toaster

**Instructions:**

1. Grate the cheese.

2. Put it in a bowl.

3. Add the milk.

4. Add the mustard, salt and pepper.

5. Mix it.

6. Slice a tomato.

7. Toast bread lightly.

8. Spread butter over the toast.

9. Spread the filling over the toast.

10. Put under a hot grill until brown and bubbly.

11. Put a slice of tomato on top.

12. Reheat and serve.

# Chinese Noodle Soup

# How to Squeeze a Lemon

You can squeeze a lemon using your hand, but it is much easier if you use a lemon squeezer. There are many types of lemon squeezers and all will generally catch any pips. Cut the lemon in half and place the fleshy part of the fruit over the tip of the squeezer, press down firmly and turn the fruit back and forth until all the juice has been extracted. Oranges, grapefruits and limes can all be squeezed this way.

# How Are Noodles Made?

Noodles are a good source of carbohydrates. There are many types. Noodles are often used in Chinese dishes and most are made from wheat flour, water and egg. Usually, the dough is either cut to the desired width and dried or pushed through a mechanical press and dried.

Remember that pasta and noodles are made, but potatoes and rice are grown.

# Stirring Hot Liquid Safely

Hot liquid can burn, so if you are stirring liquids such as soup or gravy, do it carefully and slowly. Hold the saucepan handle with your other hand, but make sure you keep the handle away from the hob. Do not lean over the saucepan, as the hot steam can burn you too.

# Chinese Noodle Soup

**Ingredients:** Spring onions   Courgette       Mushrooms
1 tsp ginger    Stock cubes    600ml water    Vegetable oil
½ lime          1 tbsp soya sauce              1 portion noodles

1. Wash spring onions, courgette and mushrooms.

2. Cut the spring onions.

3. Cut the courgette.

4. Slice the mushrooms.

5. Squeeze the juice of ½ lime.

6. Heat a little oil in a saucepan.

# Chinese Noodle Soup (cont.)

**Equipment:**
Chopping board   Sharp knife   Measuring jug
Lemon squeezer   Mixing spoon   Saucepan   Measuring Spoons

7. Lightly fry spring onions, courgette and mushrooms.

8. Add the water.

9. Add soya sauce, stock cubes and ginger.

10. Add the lime juice.

11. Bring to the boil and simmer for 2–3 minutes.

12. Add the noodles and simmer for another 5 minutes.

# Chinese Noodle Soup

**Ingredients:**
Spring onions
Courgette
Mushrooms
1 tsp ginger
Stock cubes
600ml water
Vegetable oil
½ lime
Noodles (1 portion)
1 tbsp soya sauce

**Equipment:**
Chopping board
Sharp knife
Measuring jug
Measuring spoons
Lemon squeezer
Mixing spoon
Saucepan

**Instructions:**

1. Wash spring onions, courgette and mushrooms.

2. Chop the spring onions.

3. Chop the courgette.

4. Slice the mushrooms.

5. Squeeze the juice of ½ a lime.

6. Heat a little oil in a saucepan.

7. Lightly fry spring onions, courgette and mushrooms.

8. Add the water.

9. Add soya sauce, stock cubes and ginger.

10. Add the lime juice.

11. Bring to the boil and simmer for 2–3 minutes.

12. Add the noodles and simmer for another 5 minutes.

**TIP**
Share 1 lime between 2 sets of partners.

# Danish Frikadeller

# How to Turn Food Over

Be very careful when you turn any food over in a hot frying pan. The fat can easily spit/splash-back and burn you. Make sure that you do not lean over the pan as this will increase your risk of getting burnt. There are several ways you can turn food: using a turner, a pair of safety tongs or even by using two dessert spoons. When you turn using a turner, do it very carefully and don't flip the food suddenly. If you drop the food, the fat can spit and burn your hands, arms and/or face. Safety tongs may be easier to use, but aren't suitable for all foods, for example, a fried egg might burst. Using the two spoons may be more difficult for some people, but again will avoid splash-back of fat. Whichever method you choose to adopt, remember to hold the pan handle.

# Lean or Fat Meat – Which is Better?

**Theory**

Meat has fat in it, and sometimes meat has a lot of fat in it. Too much fat is not good for the heart, and it can also lead to obesity. The fat looks white before it has been cooked. Therefore, you can see the fat that meat has in it. "Lean meat" means meat that is low in fat, and this is less bad for you. Therefore, be aware of the fat content in meat. When you buy minced pork, a fatty meat, buy the kind with the least fat in it.

# Reasons for Keeping Your Hands Clean

**Health & Safety**

It is not always enough to just wash your hands before you start cooking. Sometimes you have to wash them at regular intervals. This may be because you have touched something that may have bacteria on it, or it may be because you need clean working hands. In this recipe, you will have to wash your hands after you have touched the raw meat.

# Danish Frikadeller

**Ingredients:** 250g lean minced pork   150ml milk
Margarine   Pinch of pepper   50g plain flour
½ egg   1 small onion   (serve on rye bread)

1. Put the meat in a bowl.

2. Mix in the pepper.

3. Chop the onion finely, add and mix.

4. Crack the egg in a cup. Whisk it and add half of it.

5. Add the milk and mix.

6. Add the flour and mix.

# Danish Frikadeller (cont.)

**Equipment:** Mixing bowl  Whisk/fork  Measuring jug
Sharp knife  Frying pan  Cup  Chopping board
Scales  Turner  Mixing spoon  Dessert spoon

7. Shape the mixture into balls a using a dessertspoon.

8. Put some margarine in a pan and heat it.

9. Put the frikadeller in the pan and fry for 2 minutes.

10. Turn the frikadeller using the turner.

11. Fry for another 2 minutes.

12. Turn the heat down and fry for another 4 minutes on each side.

# Danish Frikadeller

**Ingredients:**
250g lean minced pork
Margarine
Pinch of pepper
½ egg
50g plain flour
150ml milk
1 small onion
(You can serve it on rye bread)

**Equipment:**
Mixing bowl
Measuring jug
Frying pan
Scales
Turner
Dessert spoon
Whisk/fork
Sharp knife
Cup
Chopping board
Mixing spoon

**Instructions:**

1. Put the meat in a bowl.

2. Mix in the pepper.

3. Chop the onion finely, add and mix.

4. Crack the egg in a cup. Whisk it and add half of it.

5. Add the milk and mix.

6. Add the flour and mix.

7. Shape the mixture into balls using a dessert spoon.

8. Put some margarine in a pan and heat it.

9. Put the frikadeller in the pan and fry for 2 minutes.

10. Turn the frikadeller using the turner.

11. Fry for another 2 minutes.

12. Turn the heat down and fry for another 4 minutes on each side.

**TIP**
Share 1 egg between 2 pairs. Divide the egg after you have whisked it.

# What can you remember? (1)

Do this quiz after lesson 6.

1. What does food do for us?
   It gives us nutrients     It gives us the giggles     It does our homework

2. What should you always do before you start cooking?
   Ring your best friend     Wash your hands     Put on the radio

3. Where do we get vitamin C from?
   In the classroom     In fruit and vegetables     At a football match

4. Can human beings store vitamin C in their bodies?
   No     Yes     Only in the summer

5. Why do we wash fruit and vegetables?
   To make them smell better     To clean their ears     To wash off dirt and bacteria

6. Where do bananas grow?
   In London     In the Tropics     On the Moon

7. Where does flour come from?
   It comes from wheat     It comes in a bag     It grows on trees

8. Which letter should normally be displayed on electric scales?
   ml     oz     g

9. Why is wholemeal flour healthier than white?
   It goes to the gym     It uses the whole grains     It rides a bike

10. Should you wear dangly sleeves whilst cooking?
    No     Only if they are pretty     Yes

Name _____ Date _____ Score _____

© Sandra Mulvany and Brilliant Publications     Healthy Cooking for Primary Schools (Book 1)

# What Can You Remember? (2)

Do this quiz after lesson 12.

1. What should you do if you see an open cupboard door?
   Run away                Close it                    Ignore it

2. Should you communicate about what you are doing whilst cooking?
   No, never say a thing   Yes, always                 Only if it is
                           communicate                 your best friend

3. Why can gas ovens be dangerous?
   They like to kick people   They can fill a room     They have a
                              with gas                 black belt

4. What are carbohydrates good for?
   For sleeping            For driving cars            For energy

5. What should you do if the dough becomes sticky when you roll it out?
   Add flour               Start crying                Leave the kitchen

6. What is Welsh Rarebit?
   A Welsh bunny rabbit    A type of cheese on         A rare insect
                           toast                       bite in Wales

7. What is calcium good for?
   For the blood           For the lungs               For teeth and bones

8. Should you run in a kitchen?
   Yes, as fast as you can    No                       Only if you are fit

9. How are noodles made?
   From wheat and egg      From sugar                  From recycled paper

10. Why should we use lean meat?
    It can lean against the    It is easier to fry     There is less fat in it
    wall

Name _____    Date _____    Score _____

**Healthy Cooking for Primary Schools (Book 1)**         © Sandra Mulvany and Brilliant Publications
www.brilliantpublications.co.uk          This page may be photocopied by the purchasing institution only.

# Certificate of Achievement

## Healthy Cooking for Primary Schools, Book 1

Name _____

### Is Able to

Cut Food

Put Food on a Skewer

Wash Vegetables

Remove Strawberry stalks

Spread Using a Knife

Weigh Ingredients

Sprinkle

Turn Oven on

Roll out Pastry

Use a Grill

Squeeze Lemons

Turn Food Over

© Sandra Mulvany and Brilliant Publications

Printed in the United Kingdom by
Lightning Source UK Ltd., Milton Keynes
137446UK00001B/9-56/P